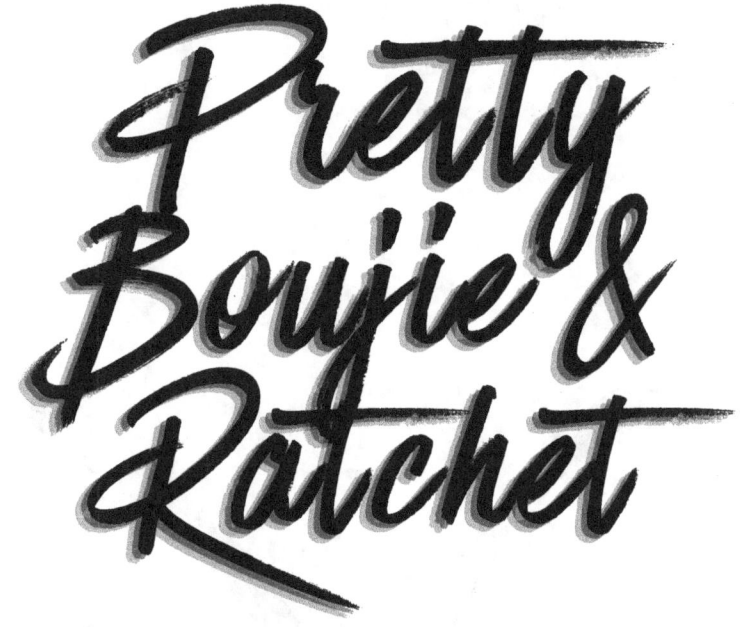

Pretty Boujie & Ratchet

Melanated Coloring

COLOR WITH GEL PENS EDITION

RELAX AND ENJOY!

Sarai "Lady Ace" Tennessee

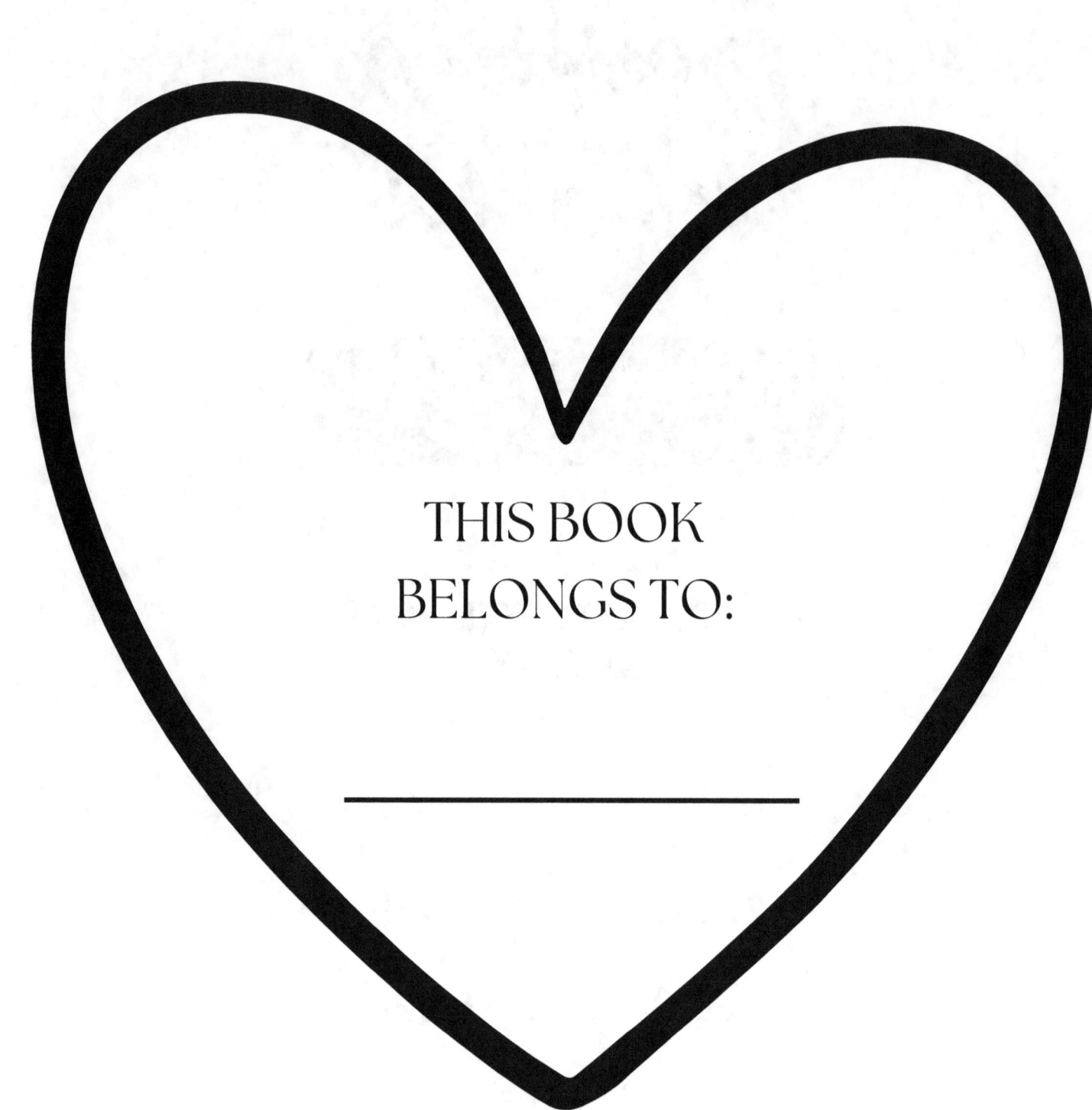

THIS BOOK BELONGS TO:

_____

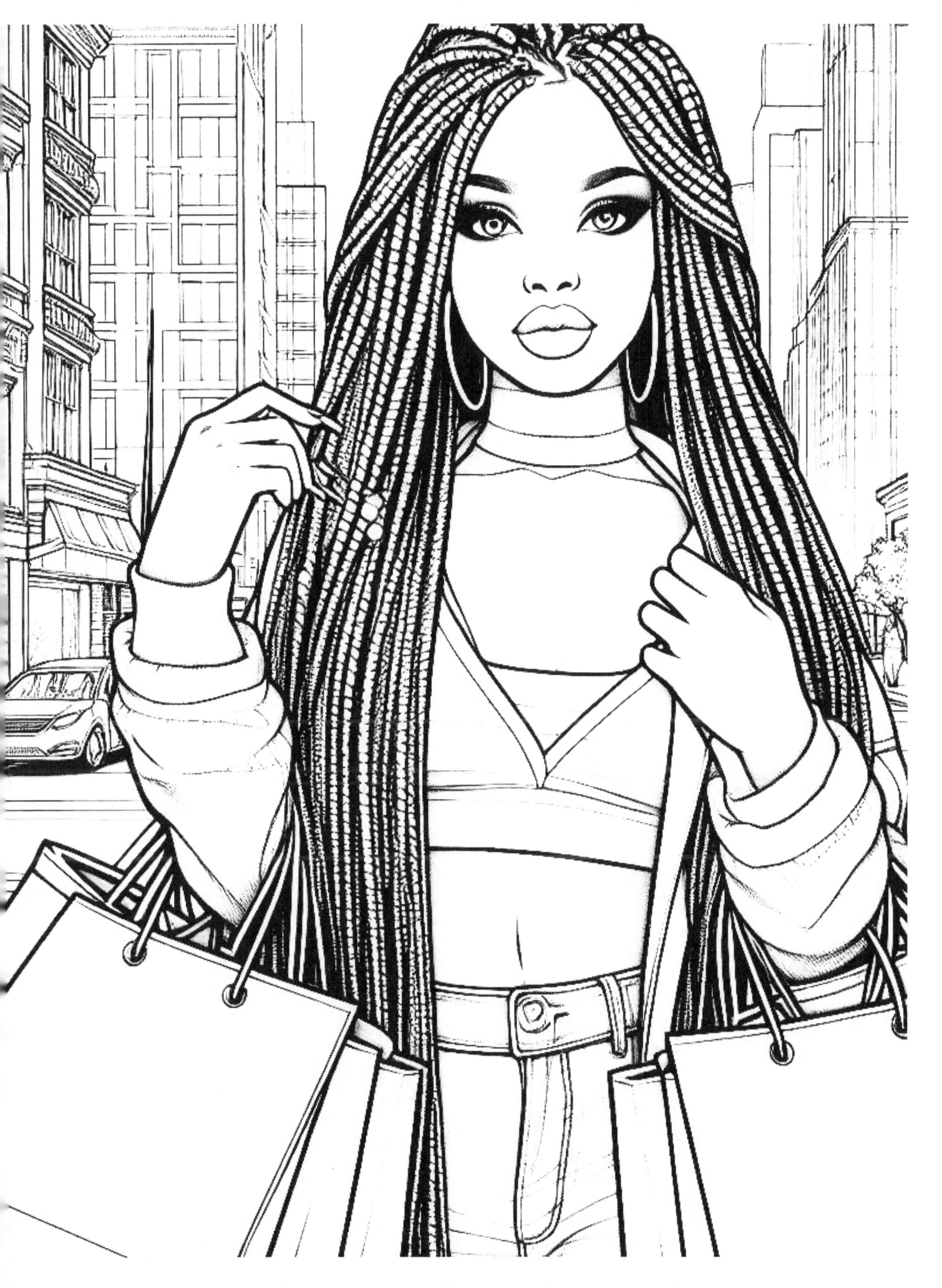

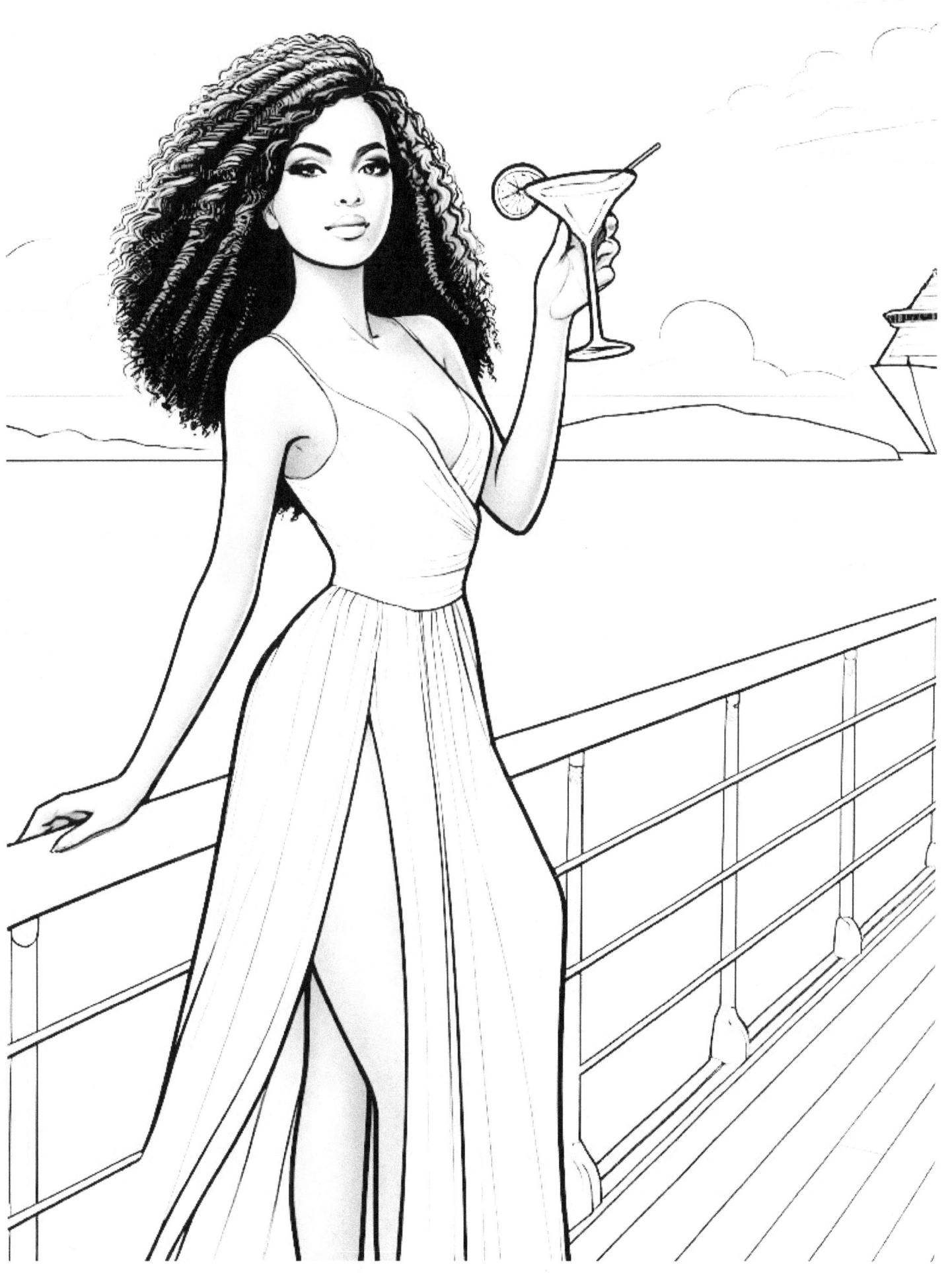

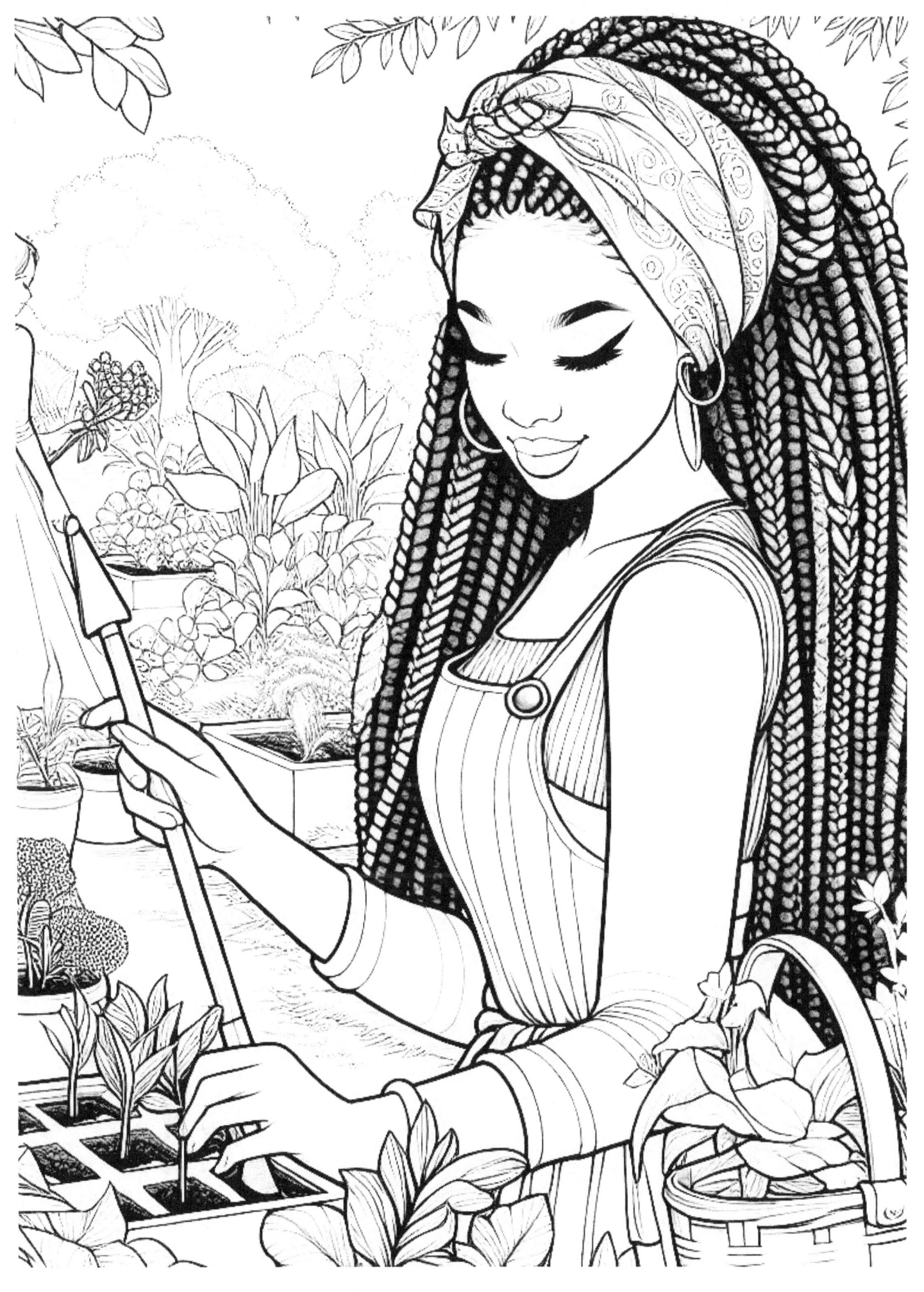

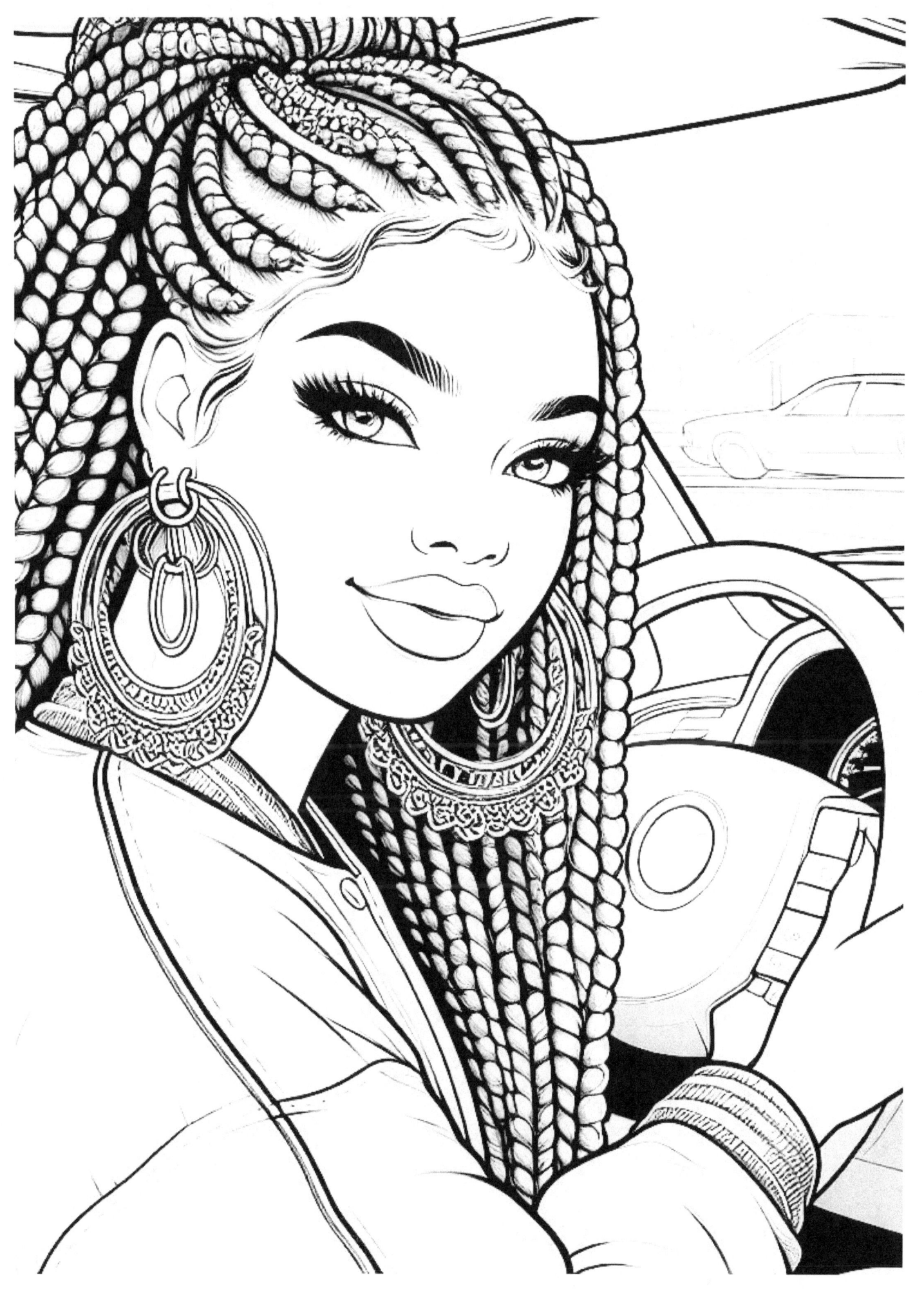

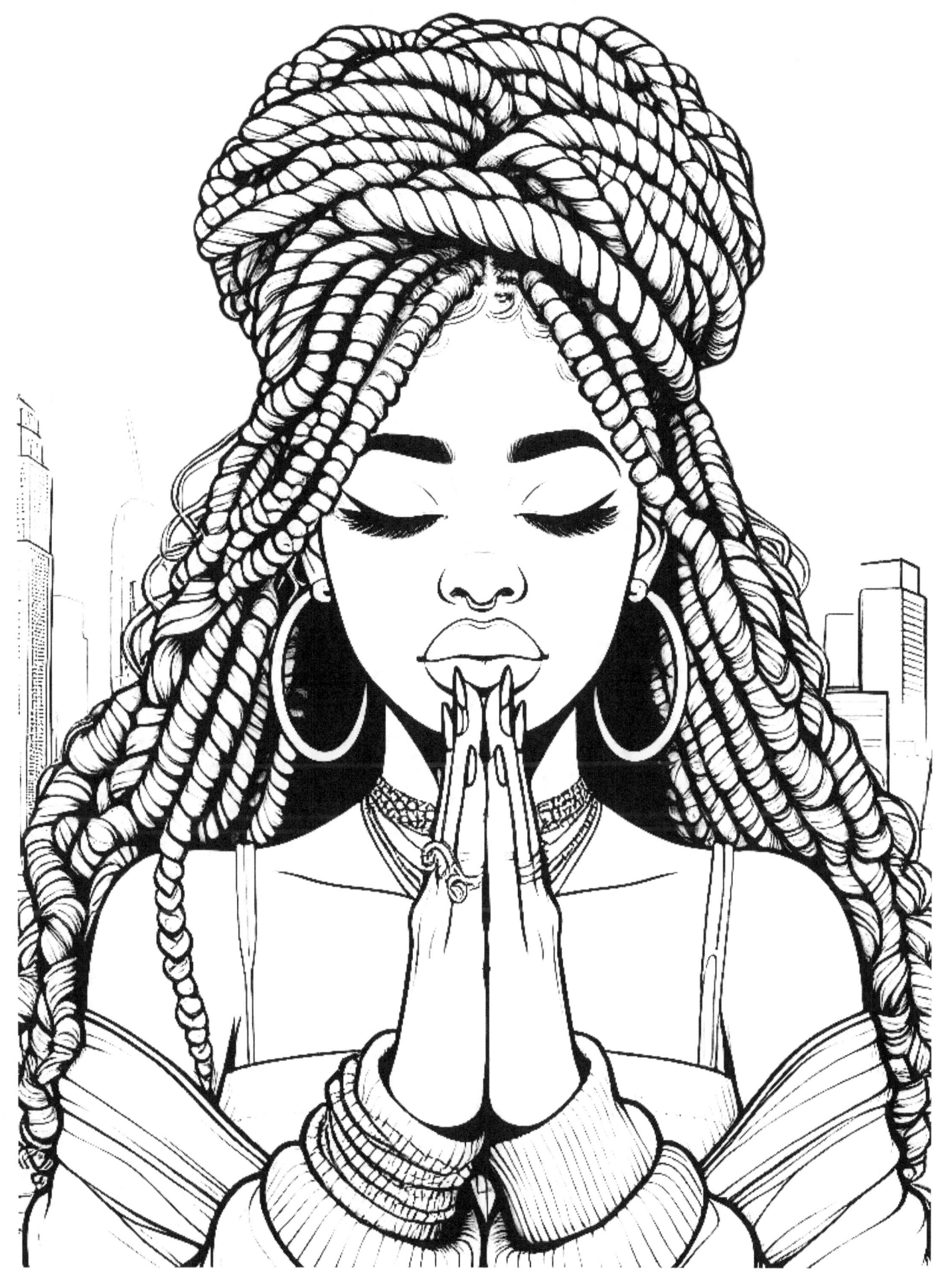

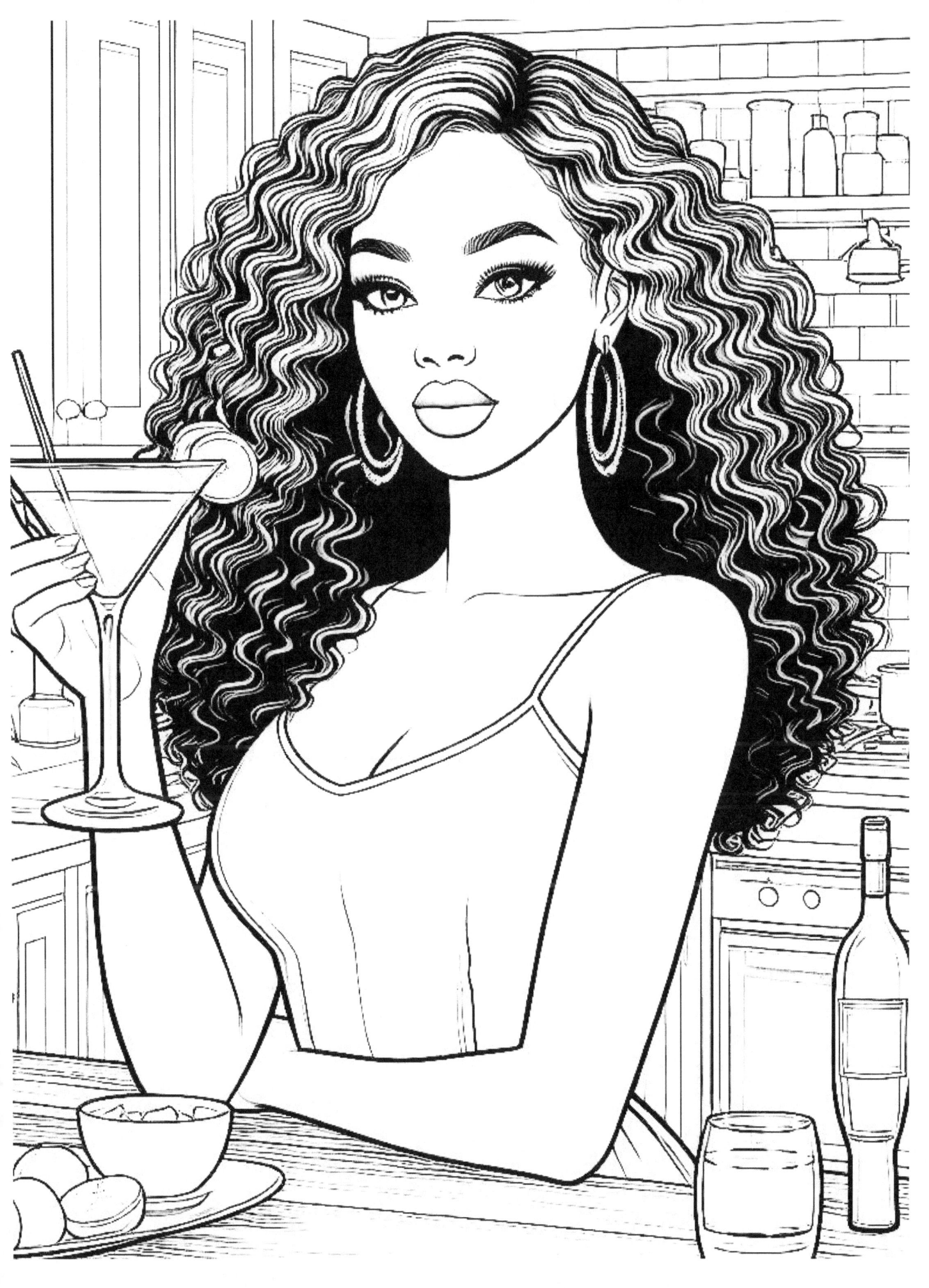

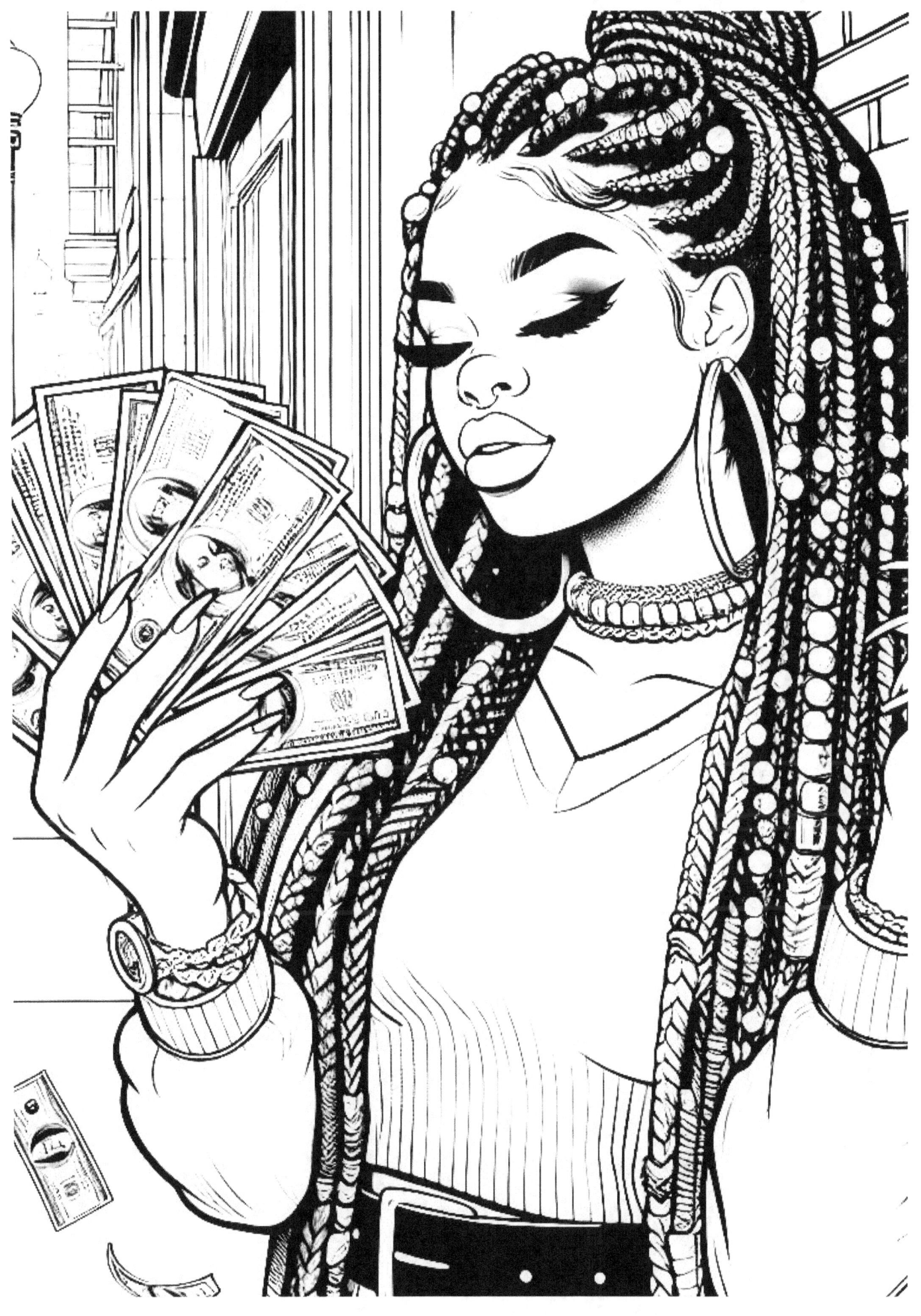

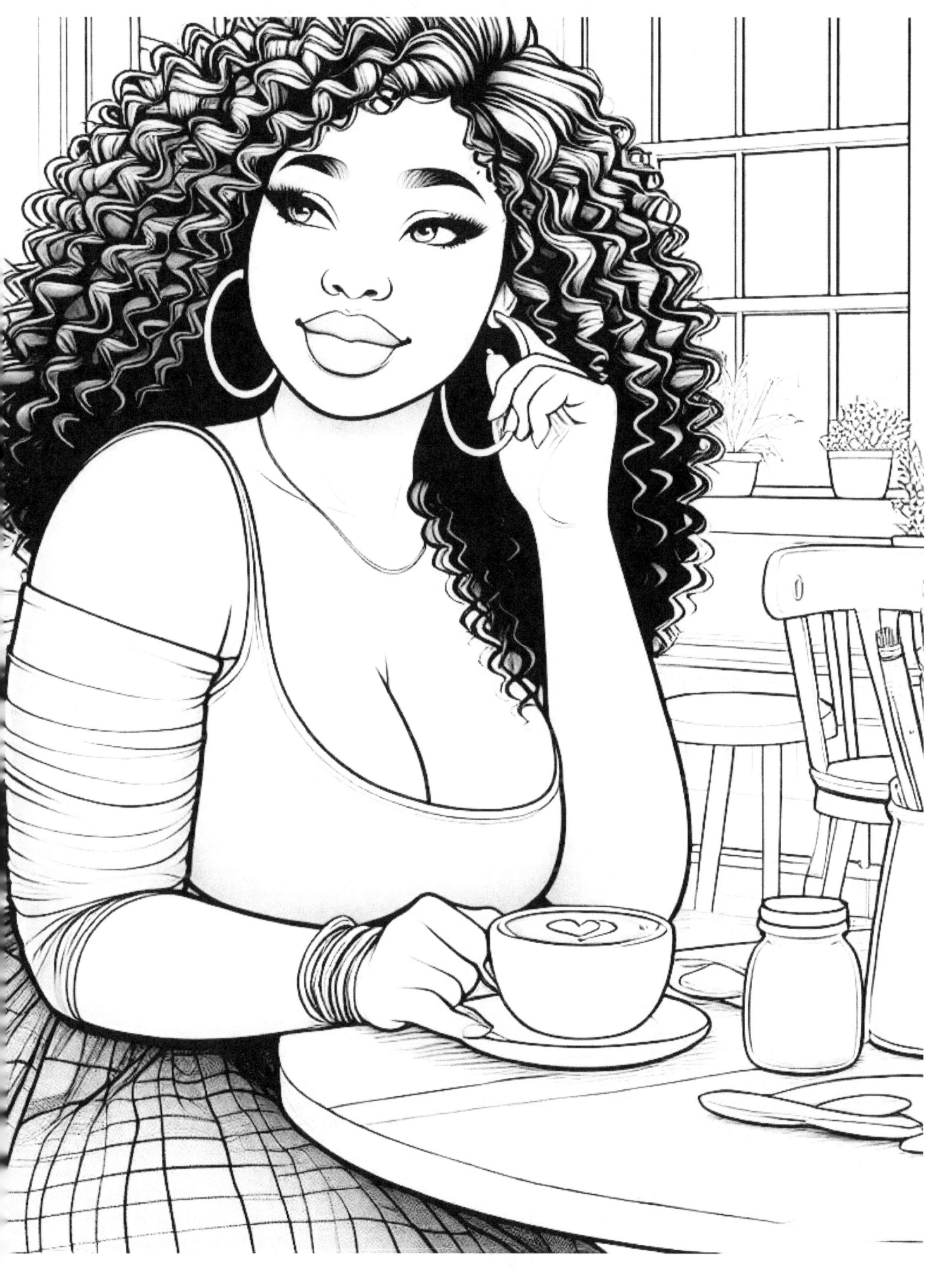

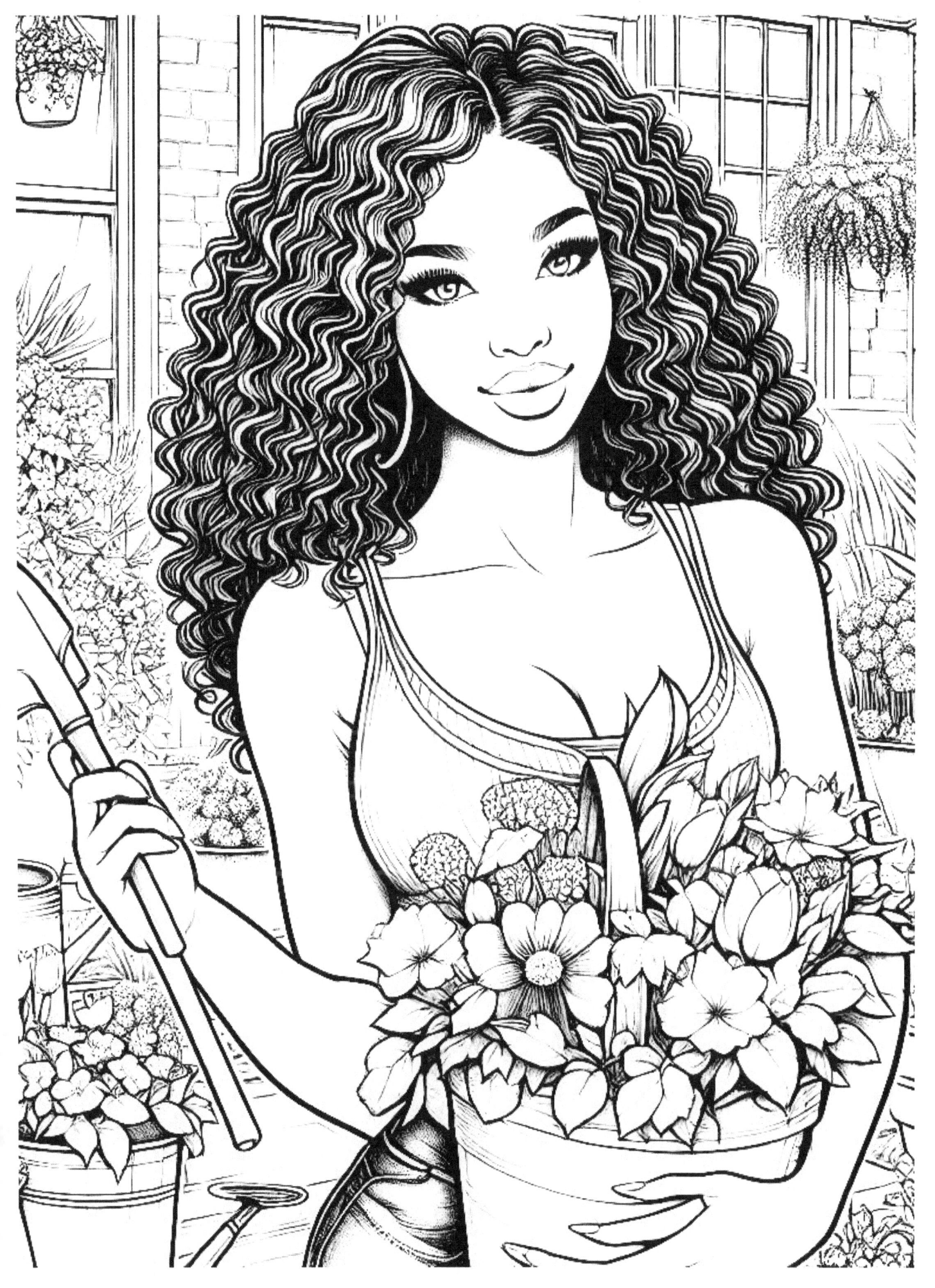

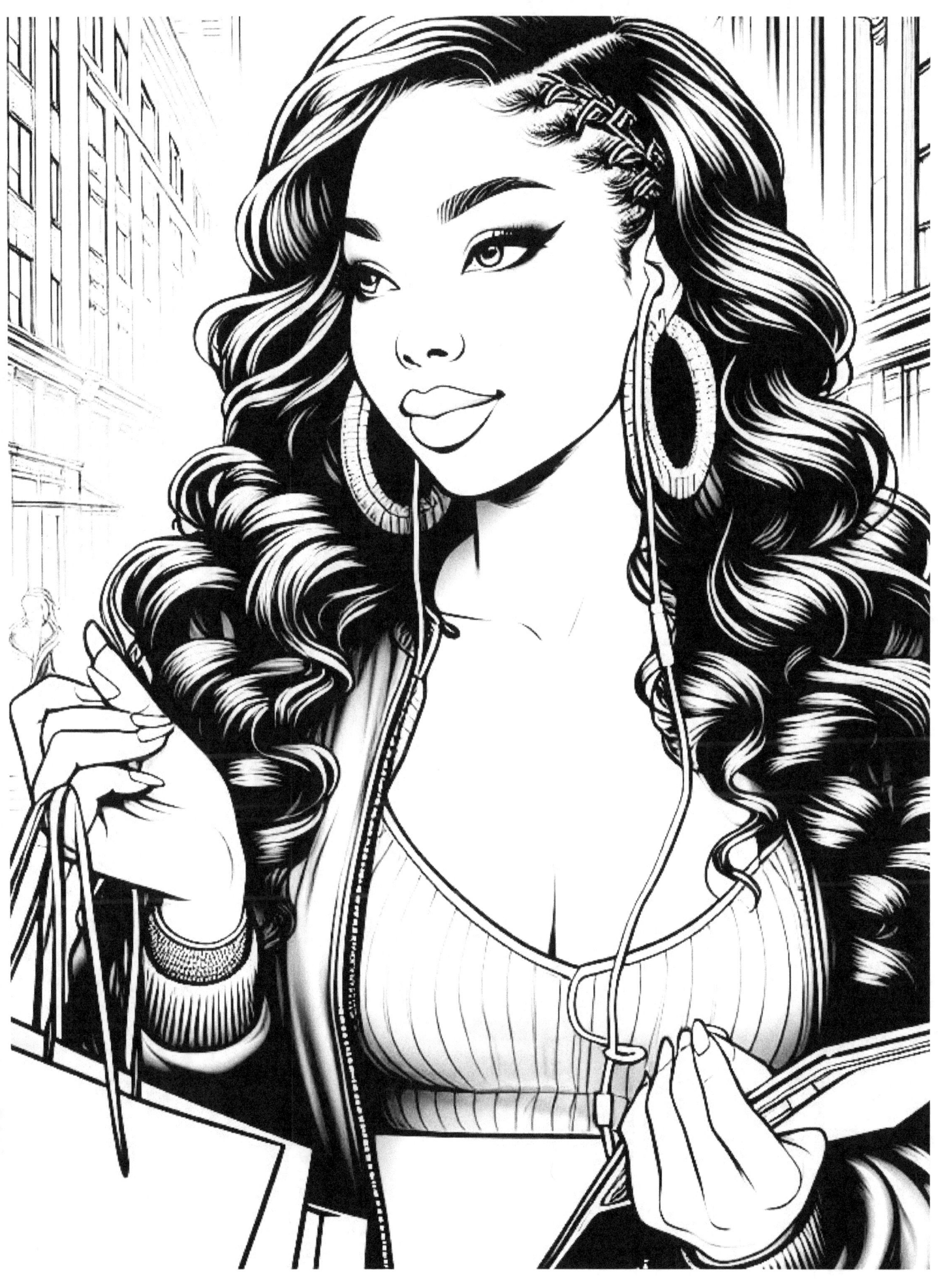

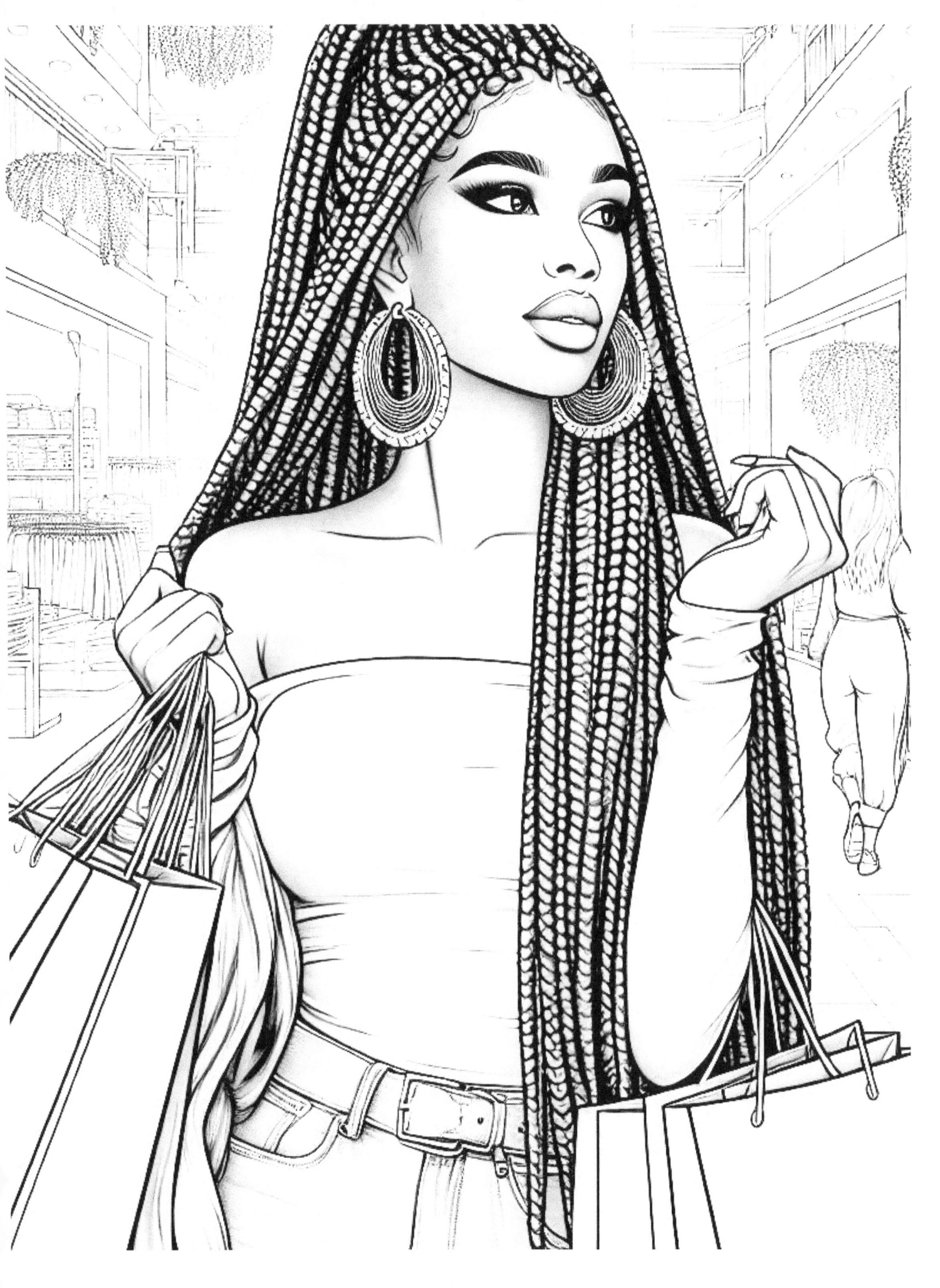

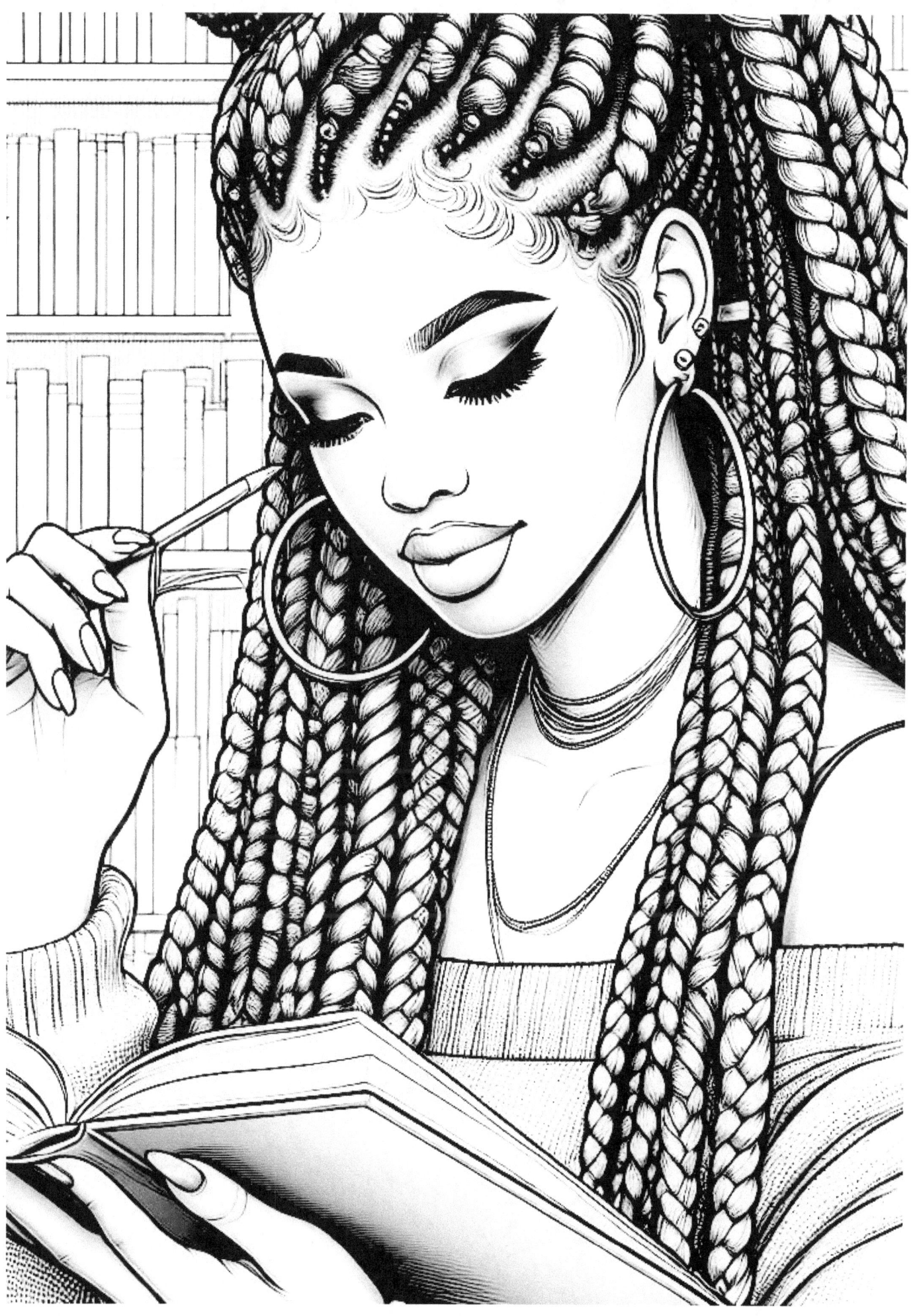

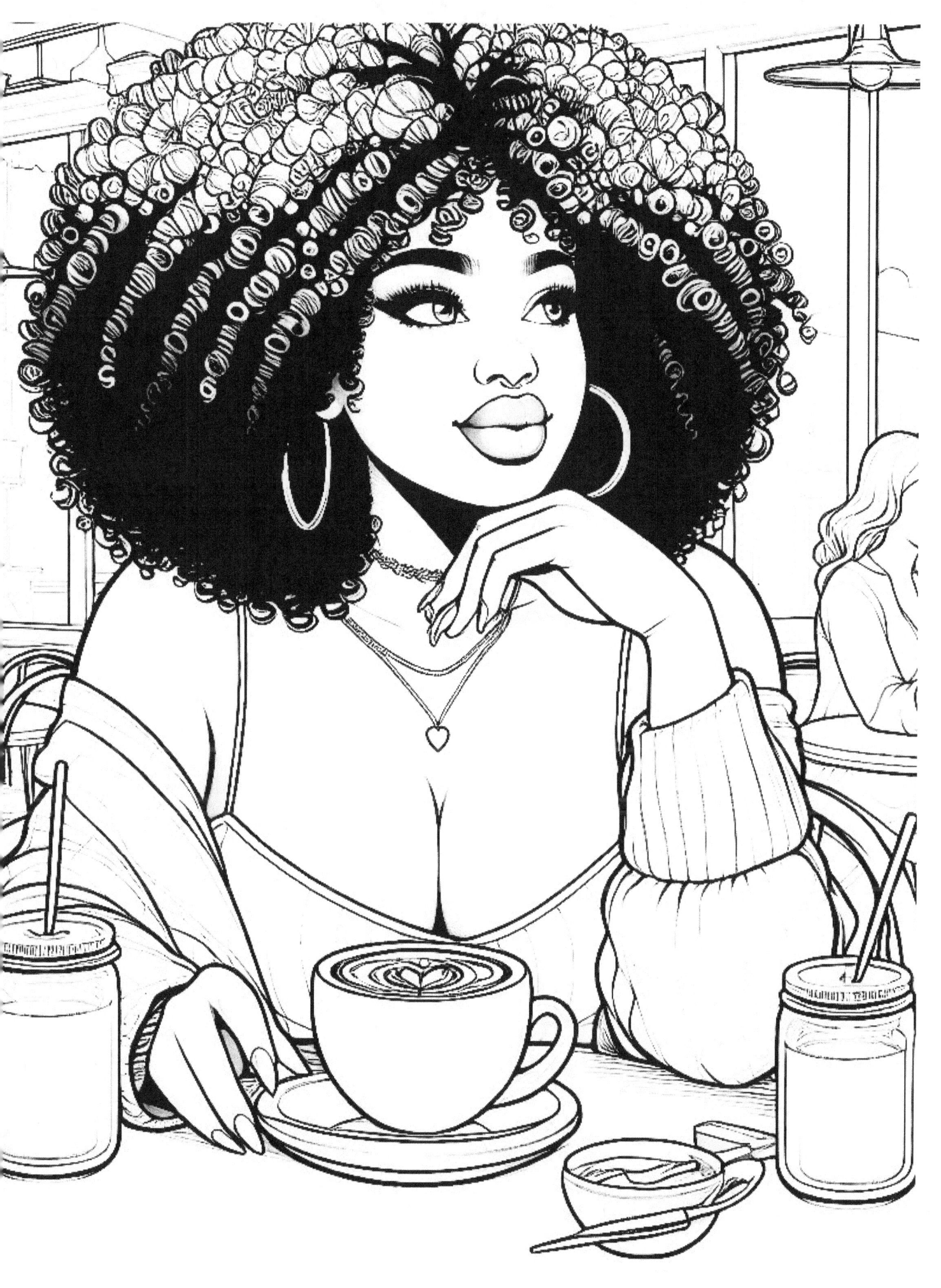

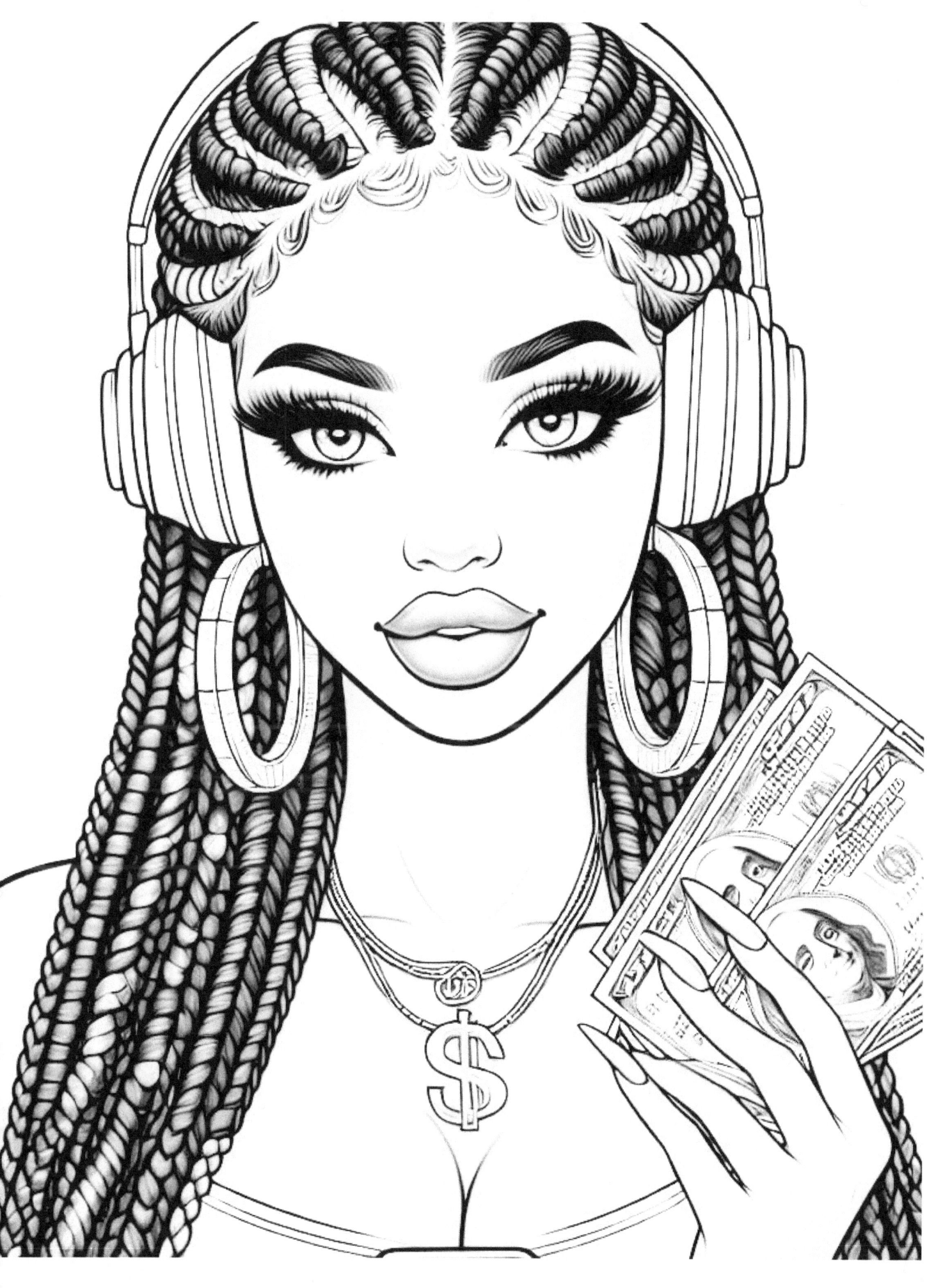

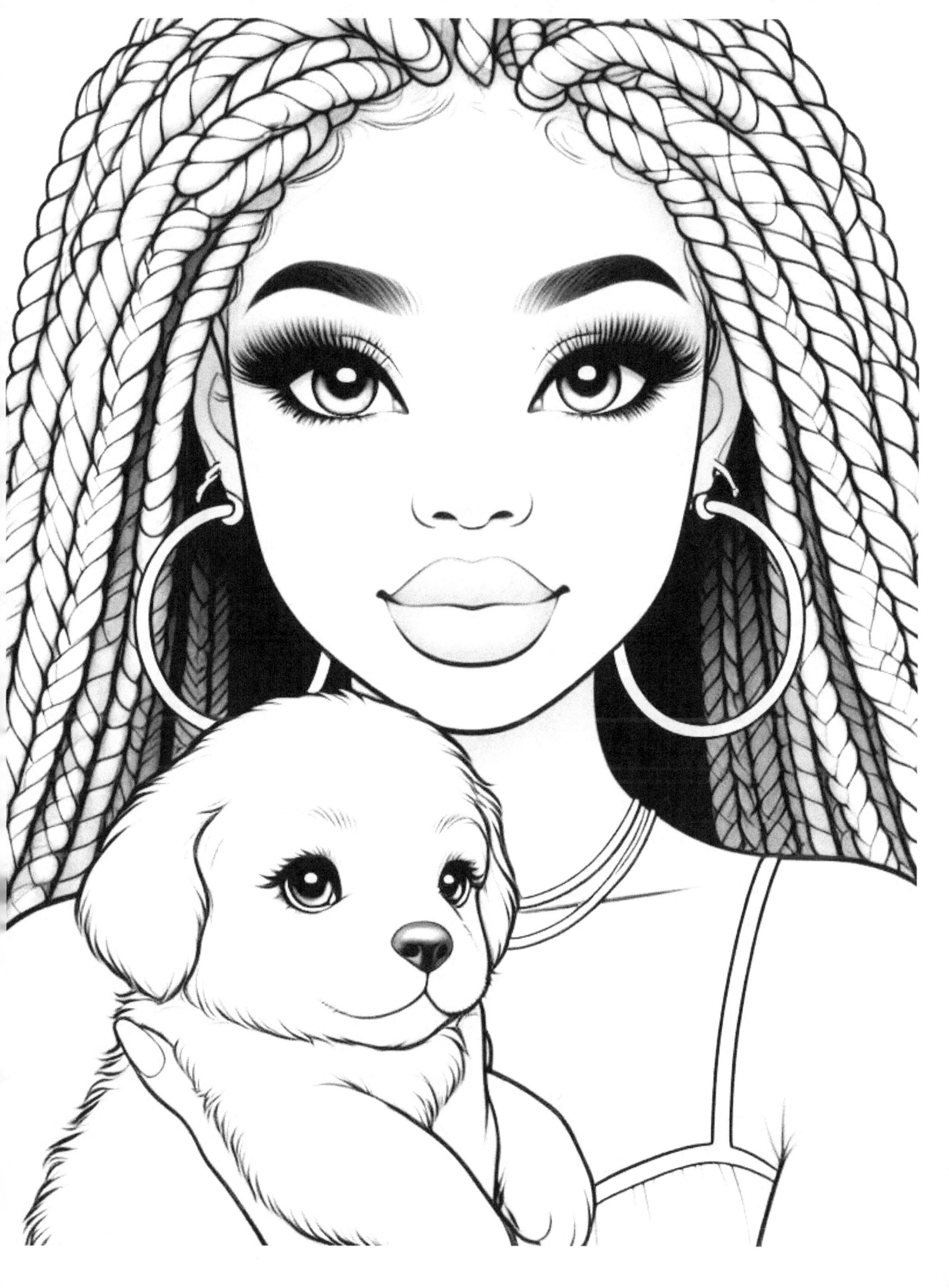

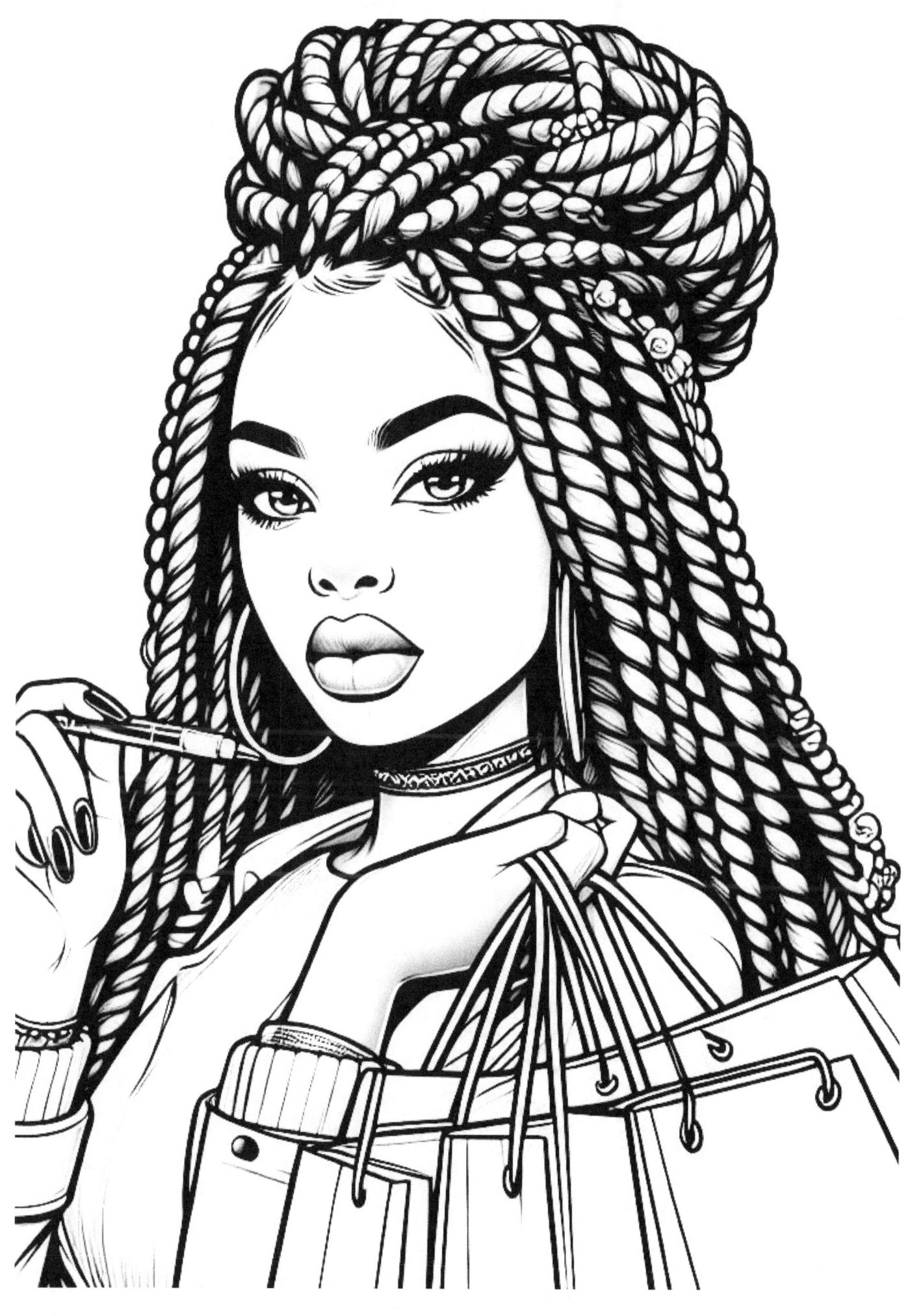

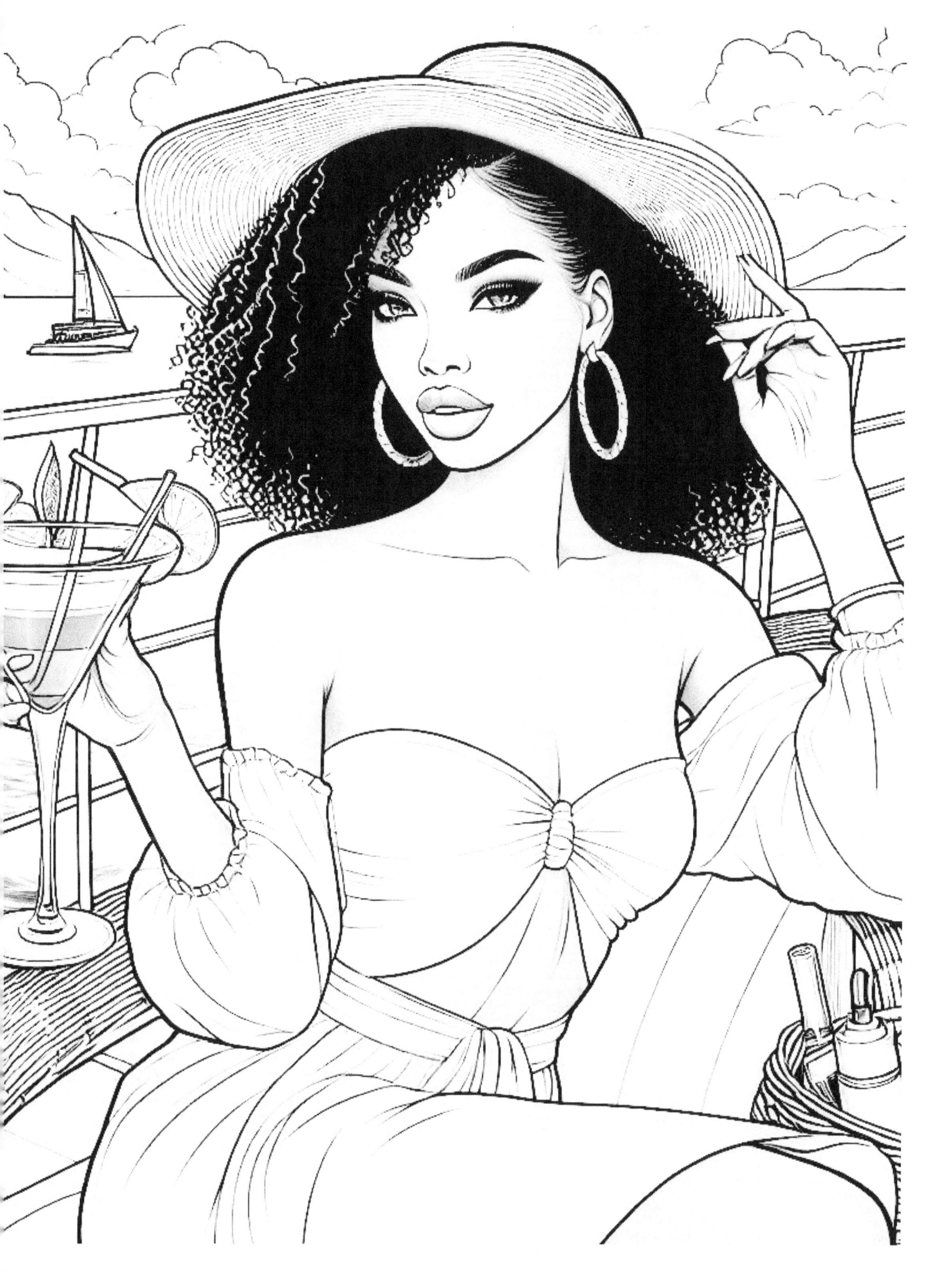

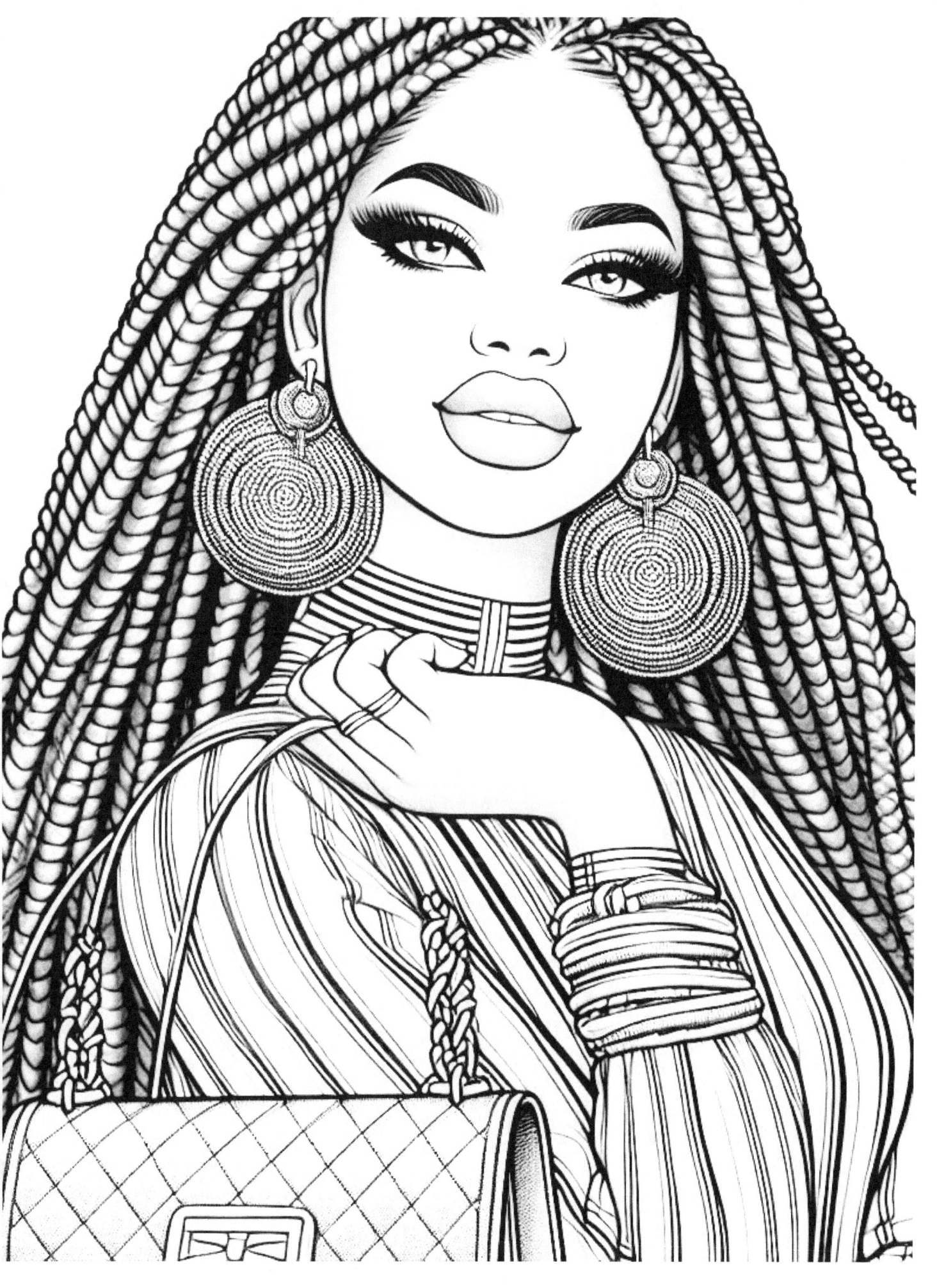

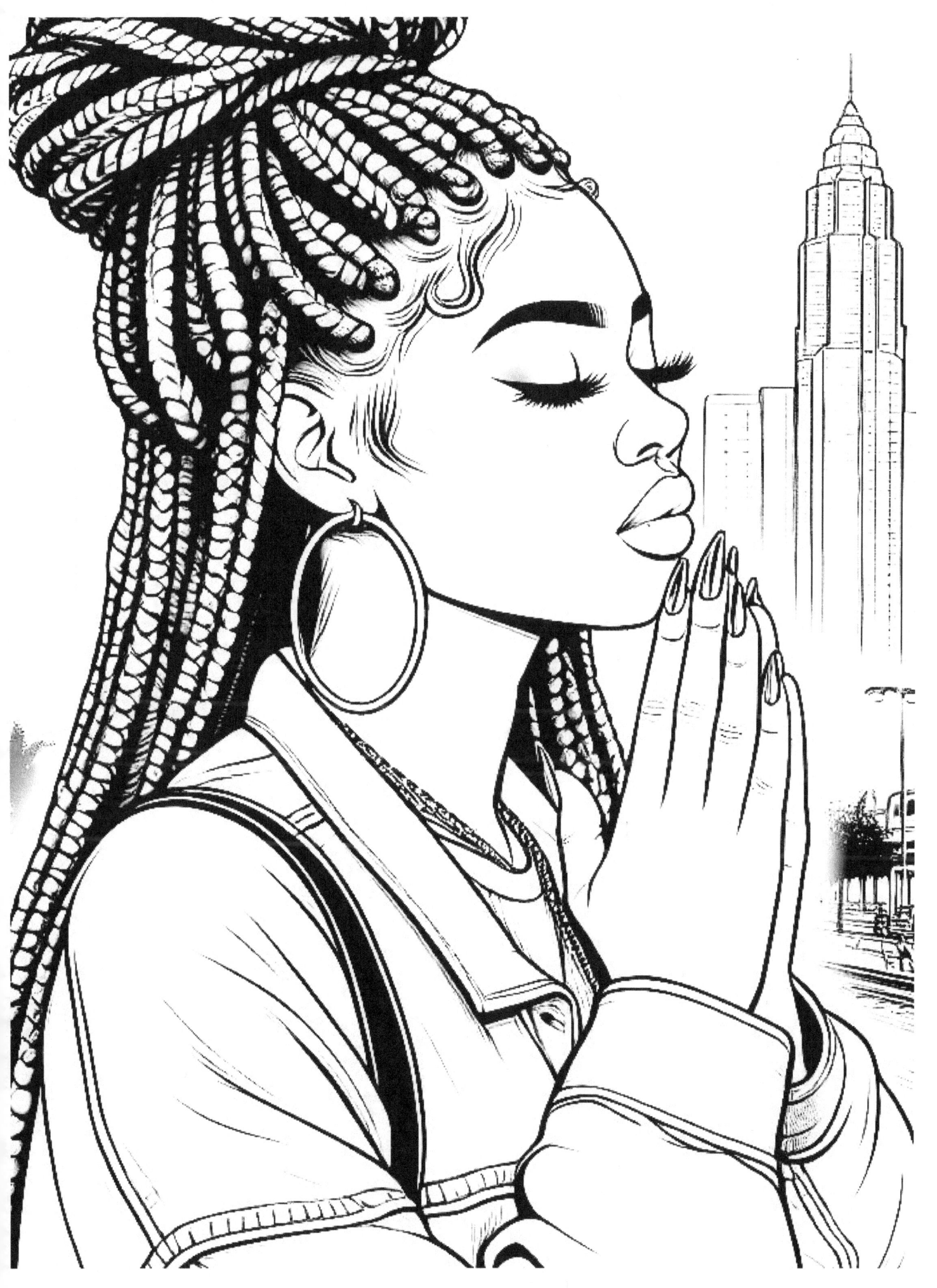

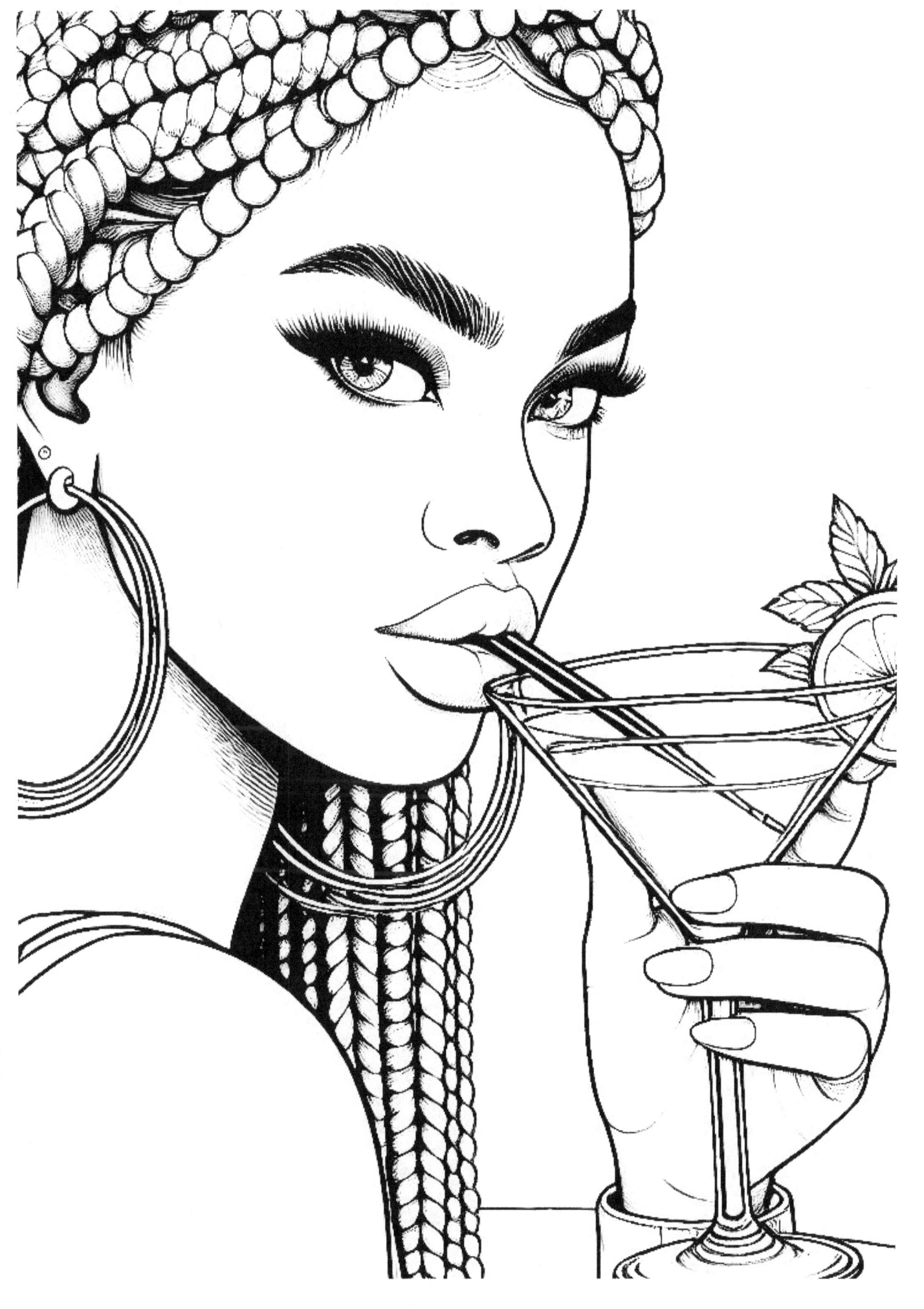

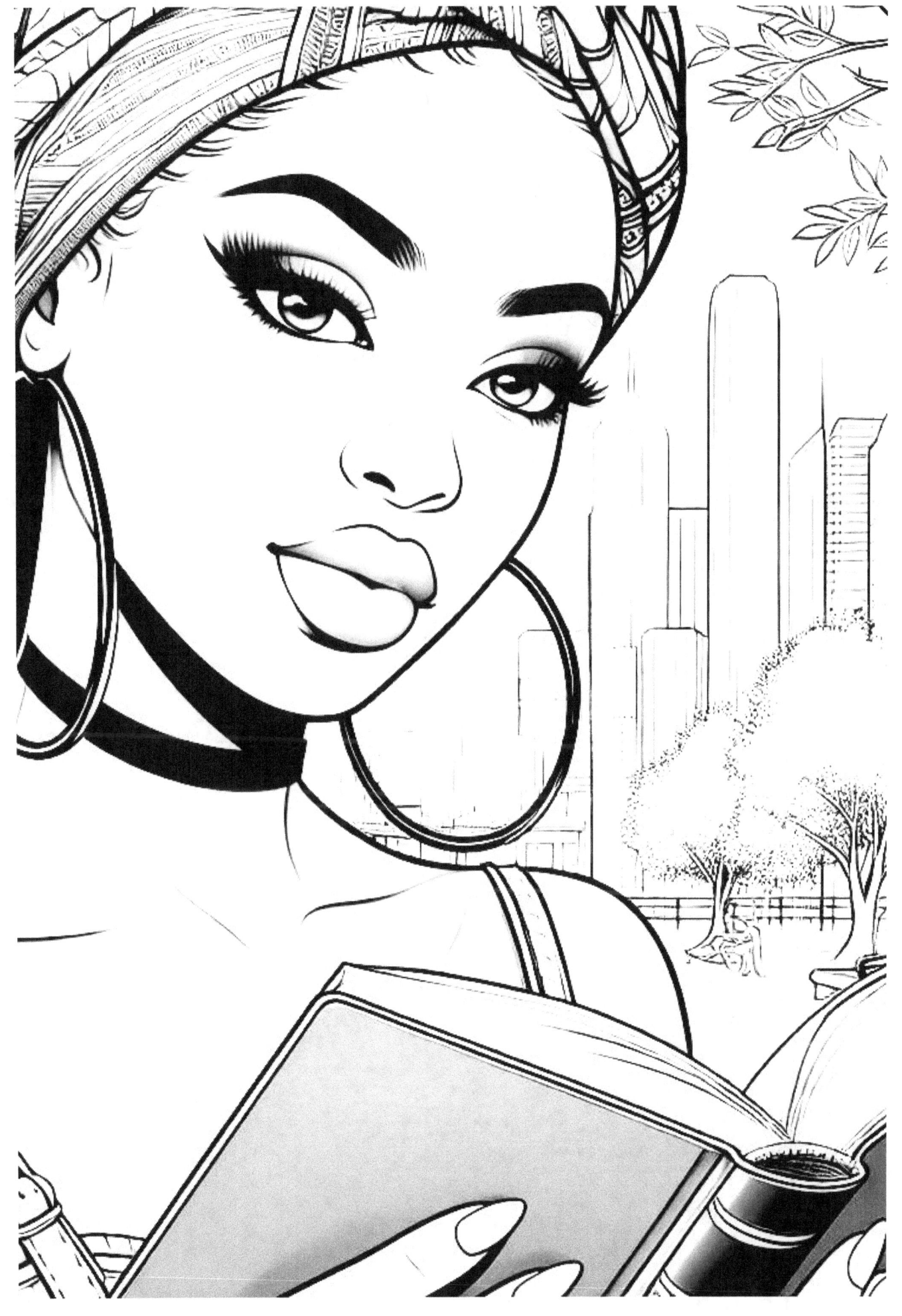

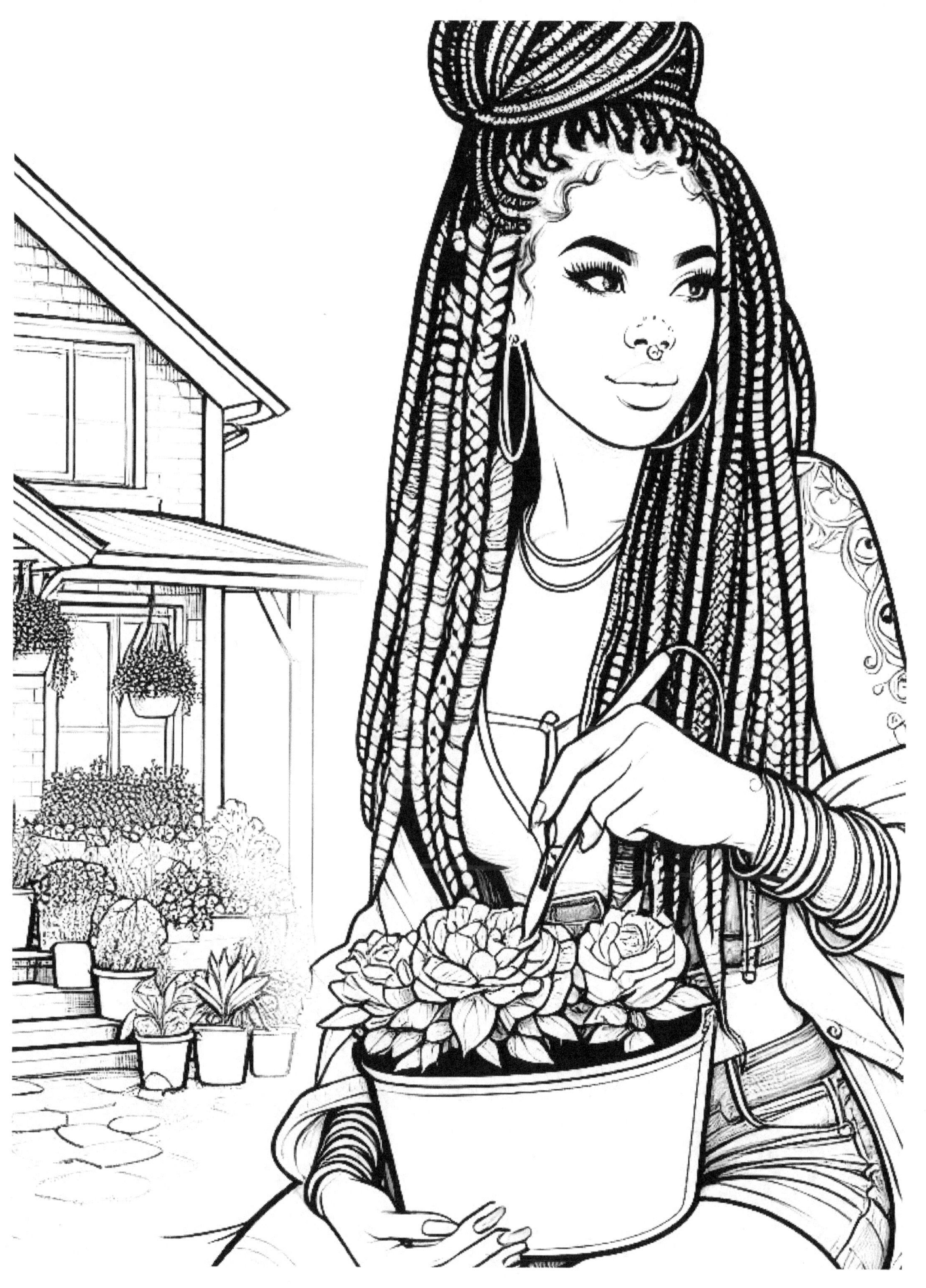

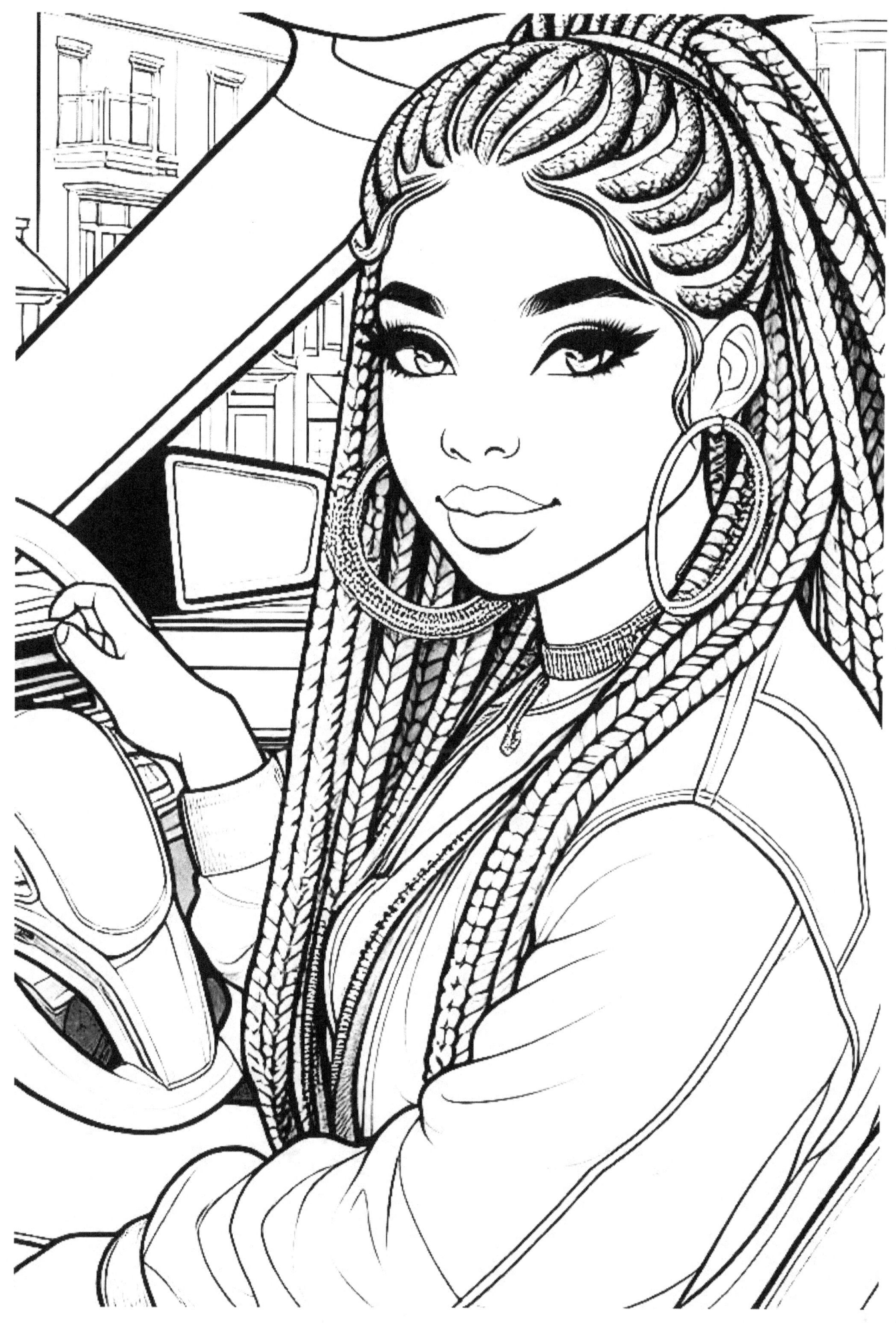

www.ingramcontent.com/pod-product-compliance
Lightning Source LLC
Chambersburg PA
CBHW081123240526
45470CB00019B/2926